G000025419

This compilation copyright © 1999 Lion Publishing

Published by
Lion Publishing plc
Sandy Lane West, Oxford, England
ISBN 0 7459 4036 6

First edition 1999
10 9 8 7 6 5 4 3 2 1 0

A catalogue record for this book is available
from the British Library

Typeset in 12/12.5 Venetian 301
Printed and bound in Singapore

secrets of

contentment

CONTENTMENT MEANS...

...love

...joy

...peace

...patience

...kindness

...goodness

...faith

...humility

...self-control

...courage

...hope

s e c r e t s   o f

contentment

Compiled by
Philip Law

Illustrated by
Grahame Baker Smith

LION
Giftlines

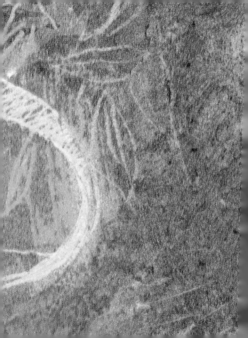

LOVE

The rarest feeling that ever lights the human face is the contentment of a loving soul.

Henry Ward Beecher

You will find as you look back on your life that the moments when you have really lived are the moments when you have done things in the spirit of love.

Henry Drummond

Blessed is the man who
can love all men equally.

St Maximus the Confessor

Only love enables humanity to grow, because love engenders life and it is the only form of energy that lasts forever.

MICHEL QUOIST

Love alone is capable of uniting
living beings in such a way as to
complete and fulfil them, for it
alone takes them and joins them
by what is deepest in themselves.

PIERRE TEILHARD DE CHARDIN

JOY

To rejoice at another person's
joy is like being in heaven.

MEISTER ECKHART

You will always have joy
in the evening if you
spend the day fruitfully.

THOMAS A KEMPIS

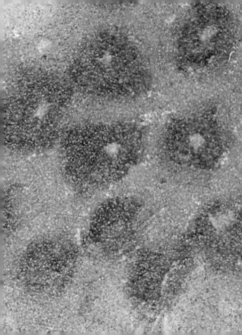

Joy is never in our power,
and pleasure is. I doubt
whether anyone who has
tasted joy would ever, if
both were in his power,
exchange joy for all the
pleasure in the world.

C.S. Lewis

No one can live without delight, and that is why a man deprived of spiritual joy goes over to carnal pleasures.

St Thomas Aquinas

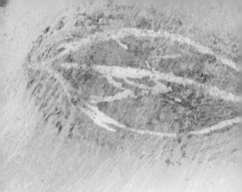

Joy is the emotional
expression of the
courageous Yes to
one's own being.

PAUL TILLICH

PEACE

Where there is peace,
God is.

WALT WHITMAN

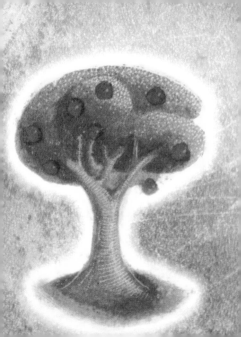

Live in peace
yourself
and then
you can bring
peace to others.

THOMAS A KEMPIS

God is a tranquil
Being, and abides
in a tranquil
eternity. So must
thy spirit become a
tranquil and clear
little pool, wherein
the serene light of
God can be
mirrored.

GERHARD TERSTEEGEN

We should have great
peace if we did not
busy ourselves with
what others say and do.

THOMAS A KEMPIS

Peace comes not by
establishing a calm
outward setting
so much as by
inwardly surrendering
to whatever the setting.

HUBERT van ZELLER

PATIENCE

He who possesses patience
possesses himself.

RAYMOND LULL

Be patient toward
all that is unsolved
in your heart.

DAG HAMMARSKJÖLD

To climb steep hills
Requires slow pace at first.

WILLIAM SHAKESPEARE

Let nothing disturb you,
nothing frighten you;
All things are passing:
God never changes;
Patient endurance
Attains all things;
Whoever possesses God
Lacks nothing;
God alone suffices.

St Teresa of Avila

Waiting patiently
in expectation
is the foundation
of the spiritual life.

SIMONE WEIL

KINDNESS

Nobody is kind to only
one person at once, but
to many persons in one.

F.W. FABER

It is better to be
faithful than famous.

THEODORE ROOSEVELT

Every creative
act of ours in
relation to other
people — an act
of love, of pity,
of help, of
peacemaking —
not merely has
a future but is
eternal.

NICOLAS BERDYAEV

Kind words are the music of the world. They have a power which seems to be beyond natural causes, as though they were some angel's song which had lost its way and come to earth.

F.W. FABER

God is revealed as the God of love, and henceforth every morally good act, that is, every act formed by charity, is a revelation of God. Every word of truth and love, every hand extended in kindness, echoes the inner life of the Trinity.

GABRIEL MORAN

I expect to pass through life
but once. If therefore there be
any kindness I can show, or
any good thing I can do to any
fellow being, let me do it now,
and not defer or neglect it, as
I shall not pass this way again.

WILLIAM PENN

GOODNESS

To be good is
to be in harmony
with one's self.

OSCAR WILDE

Good will is the source of all good and the mother of all virtues; whoever begins to have that good will has gained all the help he needs for the good life.

ALBERT THE GREAT

Genuine goodness is a matter of
habitually acting and responding
appropriately in each situation,
as it arises, moved always by the
desire to please God.

THE CLOUD OF UNKNOWING

Have a good conscience,
and you will always have
gladness; for a good
conscience is able to
endure a great deal,
and be glad even in
adversity, whereas a bad
conscience is always
fearful and restless.

THOMAS A KEMPIS

Perfection never exists apart from imperfection, just as good health cannot exist without our feeling effort, fatigue, hunger or thirst, heat or cold; yet none of those prevent the enjoyment of good health.

HENRI DE TOURVILLE

FAITH

It is cynicism and fear
that freeze life;
it is faith that thaws it out,
releases it, sets it free.

HARRY EMERSON FOSDICK

I believe in the sun
even when it is not shining.
I believe in love
even when I don't feel it.
I believe in God
even when he is silent.

*ANONYMOUS (WORDS FOUND ON
A PRISON CELL WALL IN EUROPE)*

Live in faith and hope, though
it be in darkness, for in this
darkness God protects the soul.
Cast your care upon God, for you
are His and He will not forget you.

ST JOHN OF THE CROSS

And we shall be
truly wise if we be
made content;
content, too, not only
with what we can
understand, but
content with what
we do not understand
— the habit of mind
which theologians call
— and rightly — faith
in God.

CHARLES KINGSLEY

Ultimately, faith is the only key to the universe. The final meaning of human existence, and the answers to the questions on which all our happiness depends cannot be found in any other way.

Thomas Merton

HUMILITY

If you are humble,
nothing will touch you,
neither praise
nor disgrace,
because you know
what you are.

MOTHER TERESA

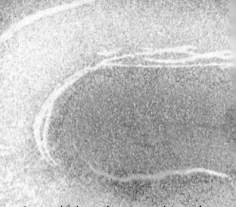

In itself, humility is nothing else
but a true knowledge and awareness
of oneself as one really is.

THE CLOUD OF UNKNOWING

All greatness grows
by self-abasement,
and not by exalting itself.

NESTORIUS

The soul of a humble
man is like the sea:
throw a stone into the
sea – for a moment it
will ruffle the surface
a little, and then sink
to the bottom.

Staretz Silouan

In the case of virtues, it is very easy to pass from defect to excess, from being just to being rigorous and rashly zealous. It is said that good wine easily turns to vinegar, and that health in the highest degree is a sign of approaching illness.

VINCENT DE PAUL

The practice of
virtue became
attractive, and
seemed to come
more naturally.
At first, my face
often betrayed my
inward struggle,
but little by little
sacrifice, even at
the first moment,
became easier.

THÉRÈSE OF LISIEUX

COURAGE

Courage faces fear and thereby masters it. Cowardice represses fear and is thereby mastered by it.

MARTIN LUTHER KING JR

There is a point with me in
matters of any size when I must
absolutely have encouragement
as much as crops rain:
afterwards I am independent.

GERARD MANLEY HOPKINS

Do not be one of those
who, rather than risk failure,
never attempt anything.

THOMAS MERTON

Courage is not the
absence of fear; it is the
making of action in spite
of fear, the moving out
against the resistance
engendered by fear into
the unknown and into
the future. On some
level spiritual growth,
and therefore love,
always requires courage
and involves risk.

M. SCOTT PECK

The courage to be
is rooted in the God
who appears when
God has disappeared
in the anxiety of doubt.

PAUL TILLICH

SELF-CONTROL

Moderation is the silken string
running through the pearl chain
of all virtues.

JOSEPH HALL

Take care not knowingly to do or say anything which, if everyone were to know of it, you could not own, and say, 'Yes, that is what I did or what I said.'

LOUIS IX OF FRANCE

HOPE

If you do not hope,
you will not find out
what is beyond your hopes.

CLEMENT OF ALEXANDRIA

We must accept
finite disappointment,
but we must never
lose infinite hope.

MARTIN LUTHER KING

Hope is itself a species of
happiness, and, perhaps,
the chief happiness which
the world affords.

SAMUEL JOHNSON